FOOLS ON THE HILL

by the

CAPITOL STEPS

LONGMEADOW
PRESS

Published by Longmeadow Press, 201 High Ridge Road, Stamford CT 06904, 800-322-2000

Produced by the Capitol Steps, 1505 King Street, Alexandria VA 22314, 800/733-STEP

Text by Elaina Newport and Bill Strauss,
with contributions from Dave Werner

Cover and illustrations by R.J. Matson

Interior design and layout by Dan Halberstein

Photos by Ken Cobb

Library of Congress Cataloguing-in-Publication Data:

Fools on the Hill / by the Capitol Steps: [illustrations by R.J.
  Matson].—1st ed.
      p. cm.
    ISBN 0-681-41676-9
    1. United States—Politics and government—1989—Humor.
  2. United States. Congress—Humor. 3. Political satire, American.
  I. Capitol Steps (Comedy troupe)
  E881.F66   1992
  973.928 0207—dc20   92-14063
                                                        CIP

Printed in the United States of America
First Edition
0 9 8 7 6 5 4 3 2 1

Acknowledgments

We dedicate this book to all the Capitol Steps' present and former Congressional employers who (a) hired us, (b) put up with our song-and-dance routines, and (c) were sometimes even able to remain in office despite it all.

They are: U.S. Senators William Cohen (R-ME), Alfonse D'Amato (R-NY), David Durenberger (R-MN), Gary Hart (D-CO), Paula Hawkins (R-FL), Patrick Leahy (D-VT), Frank Murkowski (R-AK), Charles Percy (R-IL), William Roth (R-DE), James Sasser (D-TN), and John Warner (R-VA); Congressmen Michael Barnes (D-MD), William Dannemeyer (R-CA), Ken Kramer (R-CO), Stewart McKinney (R-CT), George O'Brien (R-NY), Leon Panetta (D-CA), John Porter (R-IL), James Quillen (R-TN), Robert Roe (D-NJ), Richard Schulze (R-PA), Mike Synar (D-OK), Esteban Torres (D-CA), and Guy Vander Jagt (R-MI); and Congresswoman Patricia Schroeder (D-CO). Of the above, we owe a special debt to Senator Percy, on whose staff all the original Steps worked, and without whose good-humored tolerance none of this would have been possible.

We also extend our thanks to our colleagues on the cast of the Capitol Steps (our co-founder Jim Aidala and book contributor Dave Werner, plus Brian Ash, Bo Ayars, Dave Gencarelli, Helen Gleason, Anne Willis Hill, Duncan Hollomon, Mike Loomis, Richard Paul, Sonya Pleasant Roth, Mike Tilford, Ann Schmitt, Emily Bell Spitz, and Amy Felices Young), who have joined us in giving up many a free evening, not to mention all semblance of dignity, for the sake of comedy; to the Steps' many off-stage helpers (especially Elaine Ayars, Judy Cutlip,

Chuck Goings, John Goings, Mike Norris, Issam Tounzi, and Bernice Weissburg), who have sweated the details while the rest of us do the fun stuff; to Nancy Baskin, Sandy Darley, Alan Friedman, Dave Nichols, and other prehysterical Steppers who meant so much in our early days; to our public-TV benefactor, Harry Figgie of Figgie International, Inc.; to the many fine people at WETA-TV, KCRW, Omega Studios, and National Public Radio; to our cartoonist R.J. Matson, and our layout designer, Dan Halberstein; to Rafe Sagalyn, Cathy Saypol, and Pam Altschul, for having such confidence in this book project; and to Paul Britten, Josh Kaufman, Bill Lane, Alan Mertz, Bijan Modaressi, Harry Teter, and the countless others who have helped propel our comic joyride over the years; and to our spouses John Romano and Janie Strauss, for their fine-tuned capacity to tell us when our jokes aren't funny, and for putting up with many a late-night fax of life.

Lastly, of course, we owe our whole comic enterprise to our nation's political leaders, Republican and Democrat, who have constantly provided us with such a rich lode of material. With rare exception, they have shown us time and again the wonderfully American ability to laugh even when the joke is on them.

Elaina Newport and Bill Strauss
for the Capitol Steps

FOOLS ON THE HILL

(Let's Get) Foreword

Have you ever watched your elected officials stammering on the news, and said to yourself "I COULD DO THAT!"? Well, adding trillions to the national debt while constantly trying to find where you left your pants can be a real challenge — but maybe you're up to it. Then again, you probably discovered that, while there are many stuffy, useless Political Science textbooks, there's never been any practical self-help guide to show you, as an aspiring politician, how to expose yourself to the public.

In this book, we'll teach you that, if you want to run for office, you should be committed. Committed, that is, to a system of checks and balances. Or checks that don't balance. You'll learn to be the best candidate money can buy.

Then we'll test your unfitness with our grueling Political Ineptitude Test. Are YOU fit? ENTER THE PIT! Wherever you see a joker's hat on the page corners, you'll find one or more PIT questions. Write your answers on the two-page form in the back of the book, and send them to our Inept Judges. If our judges find you unfit, we'll send you a certificate, suitable for a frame-up, designating you as a Certified Fool, fully capable of replacing the real FOOLS ON THE HILL!

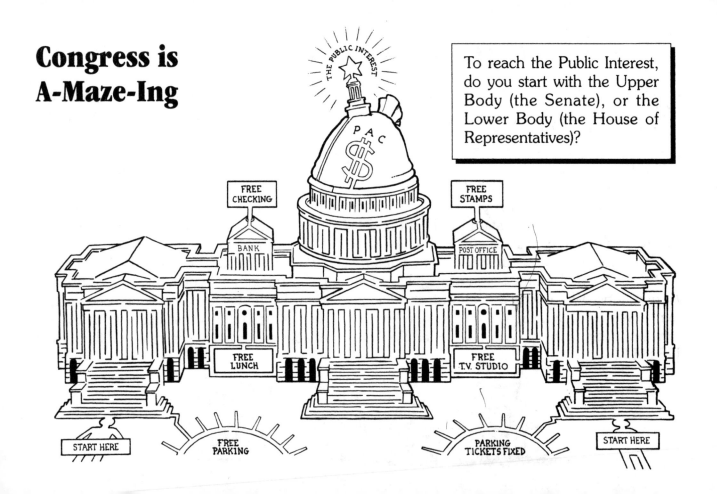

Political Ineptitude Test — Current Events

1. A former Nazi received many votes in the Louisiana governor's race because:
   (a) The other candidates were weak.
   (b) They were still hung over from last year's Mardi Gras.
   (c) There was no active Nazi on the ballot.

2. Women Air Force pilots can now fly in combat roles. This was done:
   (a) to ensure full combat readiness.
   (b) to satisfy feminist groups.
   (c) to ensure that at least some pilots won't be afraid to stop and ask for directions.

3. In recent years, which of the following has been a major national trend?
   (a) legalized euthanasia
   (b) term limits for elected officials
   (c) legalized euthanasia for elected officials

4. Salman Rushdie has been hiding now for several years. It is likely that he vanished while:
   (a) flying with Amelia Earhart.
   (b) working at a GM plant.
   (c) moving to the U.S., joining the Middle Class, then watching himself disappear during the Reagan and Bush Administrations.

And God Created Congress?
(The Book of Paralysis)

1 On the First Day God Created Congress. And Congress Said, We Are God. We Can Take It From Here.

2 On the Second Day Congress Said, Let There Be Many Committees of Redundancy, Many Men in Suits of One Color, and, Yea, a State-of-the-Art TV Studio. And So There Were. And Congress Said, May Our Staffs Be Fruitful and Multiply. And So They Did. And, Seeing This, Congress Saw That It Had Work To Do, and Set Out to Do That Work Within a Week of Three Days.

3 On the Third Day Congress Said, Let There Be Elections, and So There Were. And Congress Entered Its State-of-the-Art TV Studio and Said, Let There Be Light, and Bites of Sound, and Disembodied Heads That Talk. And So There Were. And Congress said, Let Our Opponents Be Without Funds or Mailing Privileges, and So They Were. And Congress Took the Bones of These Opponents and Cast Them Into the Sea. And Congress Was Exceedingly Glad, and Gave Many Speeches of Acceptance.

4 And Congress Saw That Yet They Were Lean, and Vowed to Do Wondrous Things. And So Congress Said, Let There Be a Large Raise in Congress-

ional Pay, and So There Was. And Then Congress Commanded the Voters Saying, These Are My Laws, and There Is Nothing in Them That Applies to Me. And Nothing There Was.

5 And Congress Said, Let Us Make Our Nation in Our Image, After Our Likeness. And So Congress Brought Forth Abundantly Among its Members Those Who Lobby, and Corps of Press and All Manner of Creatures Without Backbones, and Without Vestigial Brain Cells. And So Did Congress Create Every Fowl, and Those Who Leak, and Those Who Suck the Blood of Others, and Those Who Dwell at the Bottom of the Sea. And Congress Told These Creatures, Be Fruitful and Multiply Your Influence, But Evolve Not.

6 And Congress Saw the Tree of Taxes and the Tree of Spending, and Thought It Good That They Were Not the Same Size, Yet Both Growing Swiftly and in Abundance. Likewise, Congress Saw Itself With the Power to Cause Gold to Bounce, to Feast Freely, to Park with Impunity, and to Make Bounteous Other Perks to Come Unto Itself. And Congress Saw Everything It Hath Made and Considered It Very Good.

7 And With Such Works and Pleasures Hath Congress Continued, from Generation to Generation, Saying Unto the Voters, This Is My Behavior, and There Is Nothing to Be Done About It. And Nothing Done There Is.

You Just Don't Understate
(What Your Congressman is *Really* Saying)

Maybe you're reluctant to run for Congress because you have trouble figuring out what your Congressman is saying. That's because you never learned to speak English as a foreign language, or use both sides of your mouth effectively.

Speech

It's so good to be back here.

As you know, I am a man of convictions.

And I wouldn't have missed being here for anything.

I'm just going to make a few brief comments.

Since I first ran for the Congress, big progress has been made.

The world is a far safer place than it used to be.

Translation

What town is this, anyway?

Unfortunately, these convictions include a few felonies.

Otherwise, I wouldn't get this $2000 honorarium.

If you believe that, you probably bought Dow Corning stock.

My war chest was puny then; you ought to see it now!

In my state, no incumbent has been beaten in 10 years.

Those who used to be our enemies are now our friends.

But we must remain ever vigilant, lest circumstances change and our resolve again is tested,

And new demands placed on us all.

But we cannot forget that charity begins at home.

For now, let's take full advantage of the peace dividend.

Let's cut defense spending by half.

We need a big tax cut for the beleaguered middle class,

Financed by much higher taxes on the rich,

Because the federal government has got to learn to live within its means.

Everyone who's run against me is in debt, in jail, or in the tabloids.

Anyone who is thinking of running should check out my budget for negative advertising.

Is your check in the mail?

To repeat: I said CHECKS! Yours better be in the mail!

Boy, have I lined up swell goodies for my biggest contributors.

But not in my district, no way!

Think of all you can buy with an extra 17 cents a day!

But clever loopholes will spare my biggest contributors.

Boy, have I gotten terrific mileage off of this old punch line, over the years.

Yes, there is no such thing as a free lunch.

But we will not balance the budget on the backs of senior citizens, the middle class, men, women, and children.

By cutting back on waste, fraud, mismanagement,
We can direct more funds towards programs that really matter,
Like helping the lower classes.

You know I stand with you on abortion,

And I share your fundamental values.

Let's get tough on criminals! We have electric chairs—and it's high time we started using them.

But remember: Guns don't cause crime; criminals do.

Except, of course, in the Congressional lunchroom.

So what if that exempts everybody except affluent aardvarks?

If we triple Congress's budget for staff and postage,
Then we can jimmy ourselves another 40 percent pay raise.
Coincidentally, I graduated in the lower half of my classes.

I can't read my notes—is this the pro-life or pro-choice caucus?
Doggone it, where are those notes?
Every axe-murderer we electrocute means one less person who might someday run against me.
Criminals don't have PAC funds, the N.R.A. does.

The President has lost touch with the people.

We have a duty to provide checks and balances,

And advise and consent before we confirm any of his supreme court nominees,

Because I must exercise my constitutional duty,

And make sure the Congress functions as the Framers intended and is not bent to the whims of the day.

Democracy may not be perfect, but it's better than any other system anyone's ever invented.

That isn't to say that we can't do better.

And I will, with your help.

So that government of the people will endure, for all time.

How dare he veto the Lawrence Welk Memorial in my district!

Hey—my checkbook doesn't balance.

I confirm that my advisers made me consent to be here today.

Hey, babes: Check out my well-exercised constitution.

Term limits? That would deprive you of your God-given right to re-elect me for life!

Yeah, I know I got caught in a huge scandal, but my publicists put a decent spin on it.

Wow, was that Ethics Committee a terrific whitewash!

Third notice: Checks, guys!

I hope People and Time magazine are covering this.

"Tonight on *Oprah*, Nice Guys Who Are In Over Their Heads"

The Congre-Gorian Calendar

You may think that as an elected official, you will constantly be called in to deal with pressing issues of world politics — to deal with important global multilateral negotiations. Actually, you will spend most of your time passing bills that commemorate dates. Of the list below, try to identify which 11 are real commemorative dates actually proposed by Members of of the United States Congress. Really!

(a) Elvis Presley Day

(b) Elvis Presley Sighting Day

(c) Education Day

(d) Edyukashun Day

(e) National Good Teen Day

(f) National The-Other-Ninety-Nine-Point-Nine-Percent-of-All-Teens Day

(g) National Prune Day

(h) National Deep Doo-Doo Day

(i) National Tap Dance Day

(j) National Rap Dance Day

(k) National Fancy Footwork Day

(l) National Merit Shop Pride and Productivity Week

(m) National Stupid Lazy and Unproductive Workers Week

(n) National Girls and Women in Sports Day

(o) National Chicks and Babes in Skirts Day

(p) National Condom Awareness Day

(q) National Should-Awared-a-Condom Day

(r) Snow White Week

(s) Vanna White Week

(t) National TV Busters Day

(u) National Boom Box Blasters Week

(v) Country Music Month

(w) National I'm-a-Low-Down-Trucker-and-My-Baby-Left-Me-and-I'm-in-Prison-With-Just-My-Dog-and-My-Guitar Month

Song of Herberwauka

George Herberwauka *Bush*

In the land of Gotcha-Gimme
With the shining Ovalafis
Comes the bigwigman Sioux Nu-Nu
From the place of granite, Hamsha
Giving word to Herberwauka
To be chief, beware Raitwingas

Sioux Nu-Nu tells Herberwauka
Taking oath of Nonutaksas
Can win Voh-Tahs up in Hamsha
Then at party Nahmi nation
Herberwauka tells Raitwingas
Ridmalipsas: Nonutaksas

They make him Chief Herberwauka
Many moons of Kaindanjental
Many thousand Pointsulaitas
Herberwauka not Awim-Poh
Leading brave Irakitaki
Reaching land of Nu-Wurl-Dor-Dur

Trouble comes to Herberwauka
Deh-Fa-Sit eats all the Doh-Wup
Nation falls into Reh-Seh-Shun
Chief make trip with I-Ah-Koh-Kah
Talking trade and tossing Kuh-Kihs
Losing sight of Vi-Zhun Thing

Sioux Nu-Nu says Razumtaksas
Deh-Moh-Krets of How-Sun-Seh-Nit
See big chance for Taksumspendum
Deh-Moh-Krets say Okumdokum
To plan of Chief Herberwauka
Ridmalipsas? Ridis-Hipsas!

Raitwingas go on the warpath
After scalp of Herberwauka
After signing Law of Quo-Tah
Bringing forth the Di-ah Tribes
Herberwauka take some Ak-Shun
Kick Sioux Nu-Nu back to Hamsha

Tauk-Sho man Pat-Boo-Loos-Can-Non
Warns big chief that he will wampum
Herberwauka visit Reh-Gan
Ask for Foh-Toh-Ahp to help him
Reh-Gan tells him Wehtuh busy
Bring in star-brave Swar-Zen-Neg-Gah

Koh-Mur-Shau blames Herberwauka
For the crazy Por-Noh Moo-Veh
No more moons of Kaindanjental
No more thousand Pointsulaitas
Raitwingas send Herberwauka
Into deepest Dipumdudu

Deh-Moh-Krets want Ovalafis
Song-Gas says no San-Tumk-Lauzi
Klinn-Tunn says no Draf-Tum-Dauji
Kerr-Ree says no Reh-Sum-Loo-Tum
No one sides with Tomahawk kin
Moonbeam says to call eight hundred

All because in Gotcha-Gimme
Ahrwird shows no sign of mercy
To the poor Chief Herberwauka
After Sioux Nu-Nu had made him
Break blood promise to Raitwingas
Ridmalipsas: Nonutaksas!

Soon to be Minor Motion Pictures

Match each of these film biographies with the politician whose story it tells.

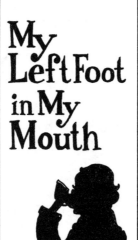

(a) Marion Barry

(b) Jerry Brown

(c) Pat Buchanan

(d) Bill Clinton

(e) Alan Cranston

(f) Ted Kennedy

(g) Dan Quayle

(h) Harold Stassen

No, Virginia, I Won't Be Santa Claus

In 1992, for the first time in memory, "Santa Claus" has become an issue in a presidential campaign. This prompted the following letter:

Dear Presidential candidates:

Please clarify your position on Santa Claus.

Virginia

See if you can figure out who wrote which answer.

(a) Pat Buchanan   (c) Jerry Brown   (e) Mario Cuomo   (g) Lyndon Larouche   (i) Paul Tsongas
(b) George Bush   (d) Bill Clinton   (f) David Duke   (h) Dan Quayle

1. No, Virginia, I won't be Santa Claus. Santa Claus is fat and spends a lot more than he takes in and thereby has eroded the basic capital investment necessary for long-term growth and cannot possibly continue these fiscally unsound policies for very long due to the lack of infrastructure and a solid manufacturing base and so we can no longer afford any more of these Santa Claus policies which we had in the eighties but those days are gone for good.

Sincerely, _____

2. Dear Virginia:

If George Bush had his way, Santa would have to live with government-imposed quotas requiring him to hire tall workers and elves with a little too much interest in the other elves, if you know what I mean! But regardless, I'm dreaming of a white Christmas.

Sincerely, _____

3. Dear Virginia:

The initials S.C. have been linked to the C.I.A., multinational corporations, the state department, Israel, and Mad Imperialist Running Dogs, and [inmate 68435's further remarks are excised, because he has exceeded his 20-word limit on outside correspondence with persons not on the approved list].

Sincerely, _____

4. Dear Virginia:

Maybe there is a Santa Claus, and maybe there isn't. I'm not ruling it in or out. And the fact that I'm not ruling it out or in doesn't mean that it's necessarily in or out. While I'm not closing the door to the idea, I'm not leaving it open either, and a half-closed door may not be more closed than a half-open door is open. And whatever I said, the press will no doubt construe as the opposite of what I said I didn't say. Then again, don't be so sure of that.

Sincerely, _____

5. Dear Virginia:

Santa Claus? Golly, what a neat idea! Just like all those funny little black lines on cereal boxes, and those socks you can buy in department stores. Am I ever impressed by all the new things people come up with these days! And I always thought expensive presents just came!

Sincerely, _____

6. Dear Virginia:

Claus was Santa ten years ago, he's Santa today, and unless we make some dramatic reforms, he'll be Santa ten years from now! He hangs on as official gift-giver, year after year, because of the ads he buys with those $1,000 contributions! His employees—all white males, by the way—all work under horrible conditions! He tolerates the ozone hole over the North Pole! And his sled! It isn't solar-powered, and it violates animal rights! He goes down chimneys which pollute the atmosphere! He doesn't have an eight-hundred number! (Did I mention that, when I was little, I asked Santa for a new Ouija Board and didn't get one?)

Sincerely, _____

7. Dear Virginia:

I like Santa's pointy little hat, even if it is the wrong color.

Sincerely, _____

8. Dear Virginia:

Forget about Santa. Mrs. Claus is the real issue. Boy, what a babe! And those elves! Whooo-eee! But I would never visit the North Pole. It's cold and drafty. I hate drafts. And enough of this Ho Ho Ho-ing for big business. It's time to enter the post-Claus era, with fresh ideas about Santa, and a new generation of polar leadership. And no, I'm not gonna stop running my negative ads on him.

Sincerely, _____

9. Dear Virginia:

You mean there *isn't* a Santa Claus?

Sincerely, _____

Many a Cross Word
(Was Spoken Over These Scandals)

Across

1. J.F.K. should have checked out the Italian names in her rolodex.

4. This stripper got Wilbur to jump into the Tidal Basin.

9. Danny's South American sex object.

12. She played strip poker with her Trump card.

13. She and then-husband John brought notoriety to (30-Down) and 35 (Across).

15. Woman seen in the arms of George Bush.

18. Initials attached to the (hottest) date in Arkansas history.

19. If ____ hadn't divorced Ronnie, Nancy would never have gotten to run the country.

20. Famous porno film; also, cause of Richard Nixon's undoing (last name).

21. George kicked her ***. Barbara said she rhymed with rich.

22. Herman's public passion.

24. A very dangerous word.

25. Hoosier hunk romantically linked with Marilyn.

26. What most people feel after seven years, Liz after seven months.

27. Where everyone said George Washington slept.

29. He said he felt "lust in his heart," and he didn't mean for Rosalynn.

31. Danny's golf link.

32. Mister Spring Break.

33. Kermit's little porkchop.

34. Whenever Mamie asked him "How about tonight?" Ike muttered, "O ____ ."

35. Site of tryst in (13-Across), and last name of comic troupe.

Down

2. This laptop item is handy for Monkey Business, eh Gary?

3. Only a back rub? Senator Robb, you're quite a Marine!

5. Wayne hunted-and-pecked, but this secretary couldn't type.

6. For her, Senator John was number... (we lost count).

7. Woman photographed looking longingly at George Bush.

8. The lady behind the blue dot.

10. She lost her appetite for Coca-Cola.

11. If you'd been married to Eleanor, you too might have said "I love ____ ."

12. John liked it hot.

14. He said "Nancy, let's do lunch." (Not to be confused with Barney.)

16. Nixon's undoing (first name).

17. Co-star of Ronnie's most famous bedtime scene.

19. Fifteen-minutes with Jim is enough to make anyone a celebrity.

21. Who Hillary meant when she told Bill "You don't bring me Flowers!"

23. What it's all about.

28. Hey Brock, how many is enough?

30. Site of tryst in (13-Across), and first name of comic troupe.

31. If you Crane your neck, you can see the Studds.

32. He started the whole mess.

Dunk the Doughnuts: We Need Some Bread

The U.S. national debt, now nearly $4 trillion, is the source of many of America's current economic problems. One way of eliminating it would be to hold a national bake sale. At 40 cents apiece, we would need to bake only

10,000,000,000,000 doughnuts,

or enough to make Americans ingest

3,000,000,000,000,000 calories,

or enough for all of us to gain **1,000,000,000,000** pounds,

for an average weight gain of **4,000** pounds per person...

... but hey, it sure beats a tax increase!

Fidel Castro, the Energizer Commie

Political Ineptitude Test: Math

1. An incumbent Congressman drives directly west at 75 MPH with a 22-year-old blonde weighing 115 pounds. At what time will he arrive at the E-Z Motel?

    (a) At 8 PM, assuming he paid a bribe of at least $250 to the officer manning the speed trap.

    (b) At 7 PM, assuming he was successful in getting an appropriation for a new four-lane interstate in a Federal Highway Bill.

    (c) Just in time to meet the camera crew from the Geraldo Show.

3. Under 1980s-style Reaganomics:
    (a) Two plus two is four.
    (b) Two plus two is three.
    (c) Two plus one is three, but can grow its way to four.

2. The nation faces a lack of growth in real GDP, coupled with rising interest rates, a reluctance on the part of major investors to rebuild the manufacturing base, which is compounding an already dire unemployment situation. The election is in two weeks. What is the appropriate sound-bite for your commercial?
    (a) What a country!
    (b) What's a GDP?
    (c) It's my opponent's fault.

4. Government experts say Social Security is self-financing because:
    (a) It is based on a trust fund.
    (b) Everyone pays, and everyone benefits.
    (c) They want to make you happy.

The Rights Stuff

As a Member of Congress, you might sometimes get a brilliant idea that you can't carry out because of something silly—like maybe the First Amendment. Back when our Constitution was written, citizens kept informed by reading, and by listening to statesmen give erudite addresses. These days, we keep abreast by watching sound-bites in TV political commercials. It's high time this march of human progress caught up with the Bill of Rights.

First Amendment: Free Speech

Congress shall make no law abridging freedom of speech, but never expect a Congressman to give a free speech.

Second Amendment: Right to Bear Arms

(1) Schwarzenegger has the right to bare arms.
(2) Smokey has the right to arm bears.
(3) Chicago has the right to the Bears.
(4) Everyone else has a God-given right to own assault rifles, machine guns, cruise missiles, thermonuclear weapons, Star Wars death rays, and gallactic supernovas for the purpose of splattering bunnies.
(5) Anyone who believes otherwise is a wimpo pervert freak.

Third Amendment: Quartering of Soldiers

Soldiers can be drawn, but not quartered. Retired soldiers cannot be nickeled and dimed.

Fourth Amendment: Search and Seizure

Everyone shall enjoy a constitutional right against outrageous police behavior, but only if some passerby happens to film it.

Fifth Amendment: Right Against Self-Incrimination

You can take the Fifth anytime and anywhere you want, except on an Exxon supertanker.

Sixth Amendment: Right to Counsel

Every Counsel has a right to co-counsel, cross-counsel, and psychiatric counsel-tation in the event the refiling of his motion to appeal his original filing is on appeal pending his appeal of his original motion to file his appeal before his original appeal can be filed.

Seventh Amendment: Jury Trial

(1) Everyone has the right to a jury of his peers.
(2) Kennedys are entitled to juries of their peers (that is, millionaires who peer).

Eighth Amendment: Cruel and Unusual Punishment

(1) Condemned persons cannot be put to death by burial under 25 tons of ACLU appeals briefs.
(2) Not even the most vicious of ax murderers can be forced to watch Geraldo.

Ninth Amendment: The "Penumbra" of Unenumerated Rights

(1) Insofar as everybody uses this amendment to argue everything under the sun, it shall hereinafter only be construed as:
   (a) Outlawing the removal of mattress tags;
   (b) Prohibiting cutting into supermarket express lines less than an hour after eating;
   (c) Legalizing abortions; and
   (d) Outlawing abortions.

(2) While that should settle all pending constitutional controversies, nitpickers shall nonetheless have the right to row or wade their way to the Supreme Court. If any such appeal is filed, complainants must submit eight copies of the brief, and one copy of an X-rated video.

Tenth Amendment: Reserved Powers and Rights Vested in The People

(1) Everyone shall have inalienable, insatiable, and incomprehensible rights, including the following:
   (a) The right to get back ten times what you ever paid into Social Security and Medicare.
   (b) The right to throw out other people's incumbent Congressmen and Senators, while constantly reelecting your own.
   (c) The right to free health care, including hair transplants, liposuction, and manicures, billed at whatever rates are necessary for each doctor to buy one Mercedes per year.

(2) These rights shall be litigated endlessly by lawyers, who shall be entitled to all rights reserved to the people, although lawyers are never reserved, seldom right, and arguably not people.

You Can Get Anything You Want At Congress's Restaurant

A History of Uncivilized Behavior

At some point in your political career, disgusted voters are guaranteed to say to you "DON'T BE A NEANDERTHAL!" That is not necessarily an insult. Looking back over time, well before the first political animals had great arguments over opposing thumbs, we can show how neanderthal behavior is quite consistent with the evolution of political lowlife.

Photozoa
Transparent lowlife, lacking in backbone, capable of surviving only in the light of artificial flashbulbs.

PAC-aderms
Thick-skinned, PAC-laden mud-crawlers, related to the modern-day leech.

Dinersoars
Bloated creatures with extremely small brains, large stomachs, and even larger MasterCards.

Primary Apes
Grunting primitives known for entering primary elections, supported by either a vicious left-wing or a nasty right-wing.

Ameemeemeebas
Self-gratifying worms that died from weak infrastructure and overconsumption.

Troglobytes
Common fossil that survived far too long and had to be eliminated by term limits, dynamite — and sometimes both.

Tyrantingsours
Ugly Dinersoars with sharp teeth, known for making screeching noises, killing airtime, and chewing up rivals.

Peeking Man
Horny creatures with unusual female-spotting ability and wolf-like whistle; invented the (all-male) club.

Summerians
Early migrating man, unsuited to North American climates, with a constant need to seek warmth and light in warmer Caribbean regions.

Senataurs
The modern political animal, typically migrating home every six years. The highest form of lowlife.

Pro-Magnum Man
Savages with overdeveloped attraction to lethal weapons, which ultimately killed them off.

Phone-icians
Applied primitive language arts, while entirely lacking in the ability to hear responses.

Pale-Gin-Antonic Man
Cavedwellers who could remain in a sitting position for long periods of time while moving only their elbows.

Roamins
Similar to Summer-ians, except they felt a more primal mating call and pursued multiple partners.

Foul Play: Who is More Overpaid?

Baseball Player
($5,000,000/year + perks)

Plays hardball

Boring to watch

Gets hit 1 of every 4 times

Owned by wealthy people

Has large groveling fan club

Seeks shoe endorsements

Tries to run home

Works seven months per year

Guaranteed contract

Defense not what it used to be

Bounces balls

Having a bad year

Member of Congress
($125,000/year + perks)

Plays hardball

Boring to watch

Votes right 1 of every 4 times

Owned by wealthy people

Has large groveling staff

Seeks PAC endorsements

Tries not to run home

Works three days per week

Guaranteed re-election

Defense not what it used to be

Bounces checks

Having a bad year

Politically Correct Sports-Team Names

Match the present-day sports name with the term a sensitive P.C. persyn would use.

1. Angels
2. Brewers
3. Bulls
4. Cowboys
5. Canucks
6. Devils
7. Eagles
8. Fighting Irish
9. Giants
10. Penguins
11. Pistons
12. Reds
13. Redskins
14. Trojans
15. Whalers

(a) Cannibalizers of oppressed bovine fellow mammals

(b) Non-renewable war-provoking pollution-creating gas-guzzling devices

(c) Behaviorally-challenged anti-Anglican Eireochauvinist Hibernians

(d) St.-Peterized sectarian ecumenical decedents of enhanced virtue

(e) Blubber-craving harpoon-stabbers of intelligent oceanic mammals

(f) Subterranean temperature-enhanced non-OSHA-complying harassers of individuals with diverse antisectarian values

(g) Follically-challenged Americentric airborne endangered species

(h) Revanchist Marxist-Leninist cold-war-mongering apparatchiks

(i) Upstanding examples of libidinally-abled progressive men assuming non-procreative co-responsibility with womyn

(j) Latitudinally-augmented animal-trapping puck-slapping Francophones

(k) Overhorned macho victimizers of passive vegetarian significant others

(l) Profit-absorbed promulgators of youth-targeted mind-altering liquids

(m) Monochromatic Antarctic victims of atmospheric ozone depletion

(n) Vertically-gifted muscularly-advantaged protohumans

(o) Precolonial deterritorialized indigenous peoples who engage in ritualistic male bonding with pigskins

Three Eggs & Ham

At breakfast time how starved I am
I always eat three eggs and ham
With bacon strips, a fried-up clam
Some buttered toast, a candied yam
And pancakes with a slab of Spam
But then I saw this diagram
Prepared by ...

"Uncle Sam I am!"
He said: "Don't eat three eggs and ham!"

"If you eat pigs and eggs from chickens
Gunk inside your body thickens
Then you'll see your IQ fall
Below your blood cholesterol

If this fatty food you're snorfin'
Warn your child: She'll be an orphan
If you eat an alar apple
Write your will, reserve a chapel!"

As Uncle Sam, ad nauseam
Described my body's Vietnam
I listened close, I can't resist 'im
So I switched ... to Nutri-System!

"Don't you try a liquid diet
Rats keel over when they try it
A mouse who drank some White House water
Gave birth to a six-legged otter!"

"All this food that's on your table
Has a most untruthful label

Grape nuts have no grapes nor nuts
Swiss are not in Swiss-steak cuts

No cottage is in cottage cheese
That tuna has no bumblebees

Your Gatorade contains no gators
No hash or pot in hash pot-aters"

Grateful, Uncle Sam, I am
You're stopping all this food flim-flam
You've driven me to such a panic
I'll only eat what says ... organic

Life is fun when you're anemic
Anorexic and bulemic
So I tofued, starved, and kiwied
I even ate Big Mac McSeaweed

I'll eat no ham, no eggs, no jelly
That protects my heart and belly
Yeah, I'll grow old, but with my luck
I'll get hit by a beansprout truck!

Clinton's Draftsmanship

Two days after getting a high number in the 1969 draft lottery, 23-year-old Bill Clinton wrote a letter to a colonel admitting that he had used his promise to join ROTC to avoid the draft. He declared himself a "selective conscientious objector" eager to maintain his "political viability" while saving himself from harm. Can a true kid of the '60s be accepted as a true leader of the '90s — and, in Bill's case, might this be part of a larger pattern of behavior?

April 3, 1959

Dear Mom:

Two days ago, a fumigation crew cleaned up my room. Neat-o! Yeah, I know I'd promised for months that I'd get rid of my old hula hoops, pick up my Mad Magazines, sort through my 45s, rip my Elvis posters off the wall, and shampoo the duck-grease out of my hair. What, me worry? Enough of this parents-always-know-best '50s scuz! The '60s are coming, and your little mousekateer is gonna let his hair down. So cool it, mommy-o! As a young rebel-without-a-cause, I have the right to decide for myself whether to clean my pigsty. I just wanted to spare myself from physical harm (from you). Besides, June, this Beaver has got to stay politically viable. As Art Linkletter says, kids do the darndest things!

Yours, B.C.

November 5, 1992

Dear voters:

Two days ago I won the election, after promising you throughout my campaign that I would give you a middle-class tax cut. AS IF! I was just a big ol' pander bear. Did I ever intend to cut anybody's taxes? Rightttt!! What an '80s thing for you to believe—and hey, dudes, wake up to the '90s! In a free society, an elected official should be allowed to decide for himself whether to fulfill specific promises he made to win votes. I was stuck between Little Rock and a hard place, and I had to stay politically viable. He shoots! He scores! Excellent! Chill out, votermeisters! Party on!

Sincerely, The Honorable Bill Clinton
President-Elect of the United States

The Senate Judiciary Committee Throws a Party

Political Ineptitude Test: Ethics

1. When should you NOT rip a tag off your mattress?
   (a) If the tag has a warning label.
   (b) If somebody is watching.
   (c) If you're tumbling on the mattress with a nude young staffer with friends on the Seattle Times.

2. If you see a cute baby girl as you're campaigning, it's OK to:
   (a) Kiss her.
   (b) Check to see if she looks like the fertility doctor, Cecil Jacobson.
   (c) Date her.

3. Your local newspaper reports that you are the most ethical candidate it has seen in years. This is a little like being:
   (a) the world's tallest midget.
   (b) more popular than Leona Helmsley.
   (c) in better financial shape than Macy's.

4. Which Congressional olympic sport got Gary Hart in trouble?
   (a) running at the mouth
   (b) straddling the fence
   (c) the broad jump

5. If your pollster tells you that you are running behind an "Unnamed Opponent," you should:
   (a) Seriously address the issues.
   (b) Change your name to "Unnamed Opponent."
   (c) Accuse "Unnamed Opponent" of having dodged the draft.

The House That HUD Built

This is the house
That HUD built

This is the spouse
Who lived in the house
That HUD built

This is the Member
Who couldn't remember
The name of his spouse
Who lived in the house
That HUD built

This is the hack
Who gave to the PAC
Supporting the Member
Who couldn't remember
The name of his spouse
Who lived in the house
That HUD built

This is the aunt
Who got a big grant
By hiring the hack
Who gave to the PAC
Supporting the Member
Who couldn't remember
The name of his spouse
Who lived in the house
That HUD built

These are the nuns
Who swindled the funds
Away from the aunt
Who got a big grant
By hiring the hack
Who gave to the PAC
Supporting the Member
Who couldn't remember
The name of his spouse
Who lived in the house
That HUD built

This is the boss
Who's hidden the loss
Embezzled by nuns
Who swindled the funds
Away from the aunt
Who got a big grant
By hiring the hack
Who gave to the PAC
Supporting the Member
Who couldn't remember
The name of his spouse
Who lived in the house
That HUD built

This is the Watt
Who money has brought
To call up the boss
Who's hidden the loss
Embezzled by nuns
Who swindled the funds
Away from the aunt
Who got a big grant
By hiring the hack
Who gave to the PAC
Supporting the Member
Who couldn't remember
The name of his spouse
Who lived in the house
That HUD built

*He just keeps
going and going*

This is the guy
Who never could buy
Because he was poor
They showed him the door
While talking to Watt
Who money has brought
To call up the boss
Who's hidden the loss
Embezzled by nuns
Who swindled the funds
Away from the aunt
Who got a big grant
By hiring the hack
Who gave to the PAC
Supporting the Member
Who couldn't remember
The name of his spouse
Who lived in the house
That HUD built

And what was this guy
Unable to buy?

He couldn't afford to buy the House ...

...or the Senate!

Letter Rip!
(When You Leave Public Office)

Given the fact that, if you are in political life, you are probably grossly unqualified for your position, it is always wise to know how to find another job. The key is a snappy cover letter. Here are some excellent examples.

Micky C's Used Party Goods

Dear Mr. Iacocca:

Please consider my enclosed resume, as I have major experience at overseeing downfall of great empire.

Sincerely,

Mikhail Gorbachev

JK, M.D.

"You'll never need another doctor."

Dear Saddam Hussein:

My friends and my government tell me that I am extremely well qualified to be your personal physician.

Sincerely,

Dr. Jack Kevorkian

Something like singing for any occasion

MV inc.

Weddings • Bar Mitzvahs
Awards Presentations

Dear Mr. Bush:

We read with interest your slogan, "read my lips." Is there an opening on your staff?

Sincerely,

Milli Vanilli

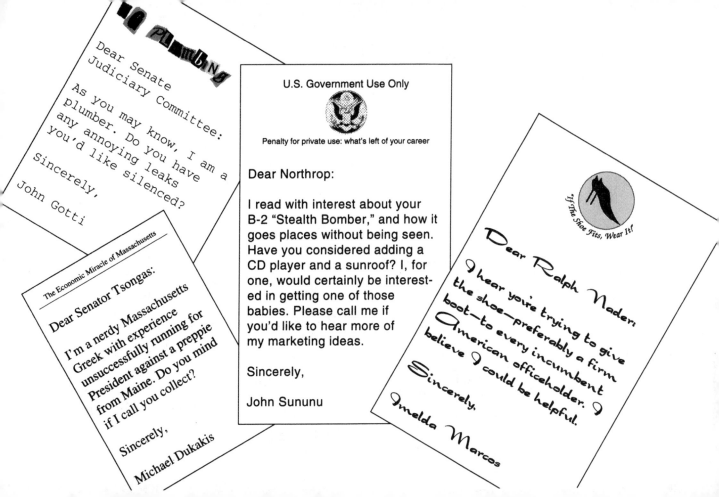

[?] PLUMBING

Dear Senate
Judiciary Committee:

As you may know, I am a plumber. Do you have any annoying leaks you'd like silenced?

Sincerely,

John Gotti

U.S. Government Use Only

Penalty for private use: what's left of your career

Dear Northrop:

I read with interest about your B-2 "Stealth Bomber," and how it goes places without being seen. Have you considered adding a CD player and a sunroof? I, for one, would certainly be interested in getting one of those babies. Please call me if you'd like to hear more of my marketing ideas.

Sincerely,

John Sununu

The Economic Miracle of Massachusetts

Dear Senator Tsongas:

I'm a nerdy Massachusetts Greek with experience unsuccessfully running for President against a preppie from Maine. Do you mind if I call you collect?

Sincerely,

Michael Dukakis

"If The Shoe Fits, Wear It!"

Dear Ralph Nader:

I hear you're trying to give the shoe—preferably a firm boot—to every incumbent American officeholder. I believe I could be helpful.

Sincerely,

Imelda Marcos

Resume Mucho

I. M. Bezzle
Temporary Address
Cellblock C
Leavenworth, Kansas

Position Sought
Account Administrator, Bank of the House of Representatives

Career Goals
Seeking a position with real challenge, such as not getting caught.

Education
B.S., Yugo School of Engineering
M.B.A., Pete Rose School of Risk Management
Ph.D., Mike Milken Institute of Ethics

Experience
Cost Control Expert, United Way of America
Manager, Lincoln Savings and Loan
Marketing Director, Pan Am
Supertanker Captain, Exxon
Political Consultant, Dukakis for President
Marriage Counselor, Elizabeth Taylor

References
To be provided upon request to Mr. Bush*

Special Skills
Ability to look the other way
Not constrained by principle

* Neil, that is

A Real Perot in the White House
(If Ross Were Boss)

1992 Stumper Bickers

To boost your name recognition, you can either get in a scandal—or pass out buttons, bumper-stickers, and placards—or both. Here are some examples not to follow.

Political Ineptitude Test: Politics

1. In any political speech, it is important not to insult:
   (a) senior citizens
   (b) your biggest contributors
   (c) Tammy Wynette

2. If you promise to create jobs, remember that:
   (a) You should be ready with specifics.
   (b) The first job you create should be your own.
   (c) You should never promise that the jobs will actually be in this country.

3. You should memorize by heart:
   (a) the Pledge of Allegiance
   (b) Your House bank account number
   (c) the 900 number for nude mud-wrestling slave nymphos

4. Which of the following is the catchiest slogan?
   (a) Elect me.
   (b) Elect me to put America to work.
   (c) Elect me to put a future ex-convict to work.

5. The most useful way to use "negatives" in a political advertising campaign is to:
   (a) go negative before your opponent does.
   (b) go negative while sanctimoniously demanding that your opponent stop going negative.
   (c) hire an undercover photographer, then print his negatives.

What Were They Thinkoln?

Here's what the following people would say if they ever dropped by Gettysburg, PA:

Joe Biden: The Get-a-Quote Address

Fourscore and seven years ago our fathers brought forth upon this continent a new nation, conceived in liberty, and dedicated to the proposition that all men are created equal. Now we are engaged in a great civil war, testing whether that nation, or any nation so conceived and so dedicated, can long endure.

We are met on a great battlefield of that war…. It is altogether fitting and proper that we should do this. But in a larger sense we cannot dedicate, we cannot consecrate, we cannot hallow this ground…. The world will little note, nor long remember, what we say here, but it can never forget what they did here…

It is rather for us to be here dedicated to the great task remaining before us—that from these honored dead we take increased devotion to that cause for which they gave the last full measure of devotion—that we here highly resolve that these dead shall not have died in vain—that this nation, under God, shall have a new birth of freedom—and that government of the people, by the people, for the people, shall not perish from the earth.

Jane Fonda: The Get-P.C. Address

Four wars and seven jeers ago, dead white males imposed upon the pristine wilderness and indigenous peoples a corrupt enterprise, achieved in jibberish, and perpetrated over the opposition of all who were not treated equal. Then these chauvinists engaged in a livid war, testing whether that abomination, or any abberation so conceited and so overrated, can cheat the poor.

We are battling with the media on this score.... We are altogether spitting on the propertied that could do this. But in a larger sense we can deprecate, we can castigate, we can be callous on these grounds.... The world will grab the throat and soon dismember whom we flay here, and we can never forgive what they did, hear?...

We are lathered to cuss and see here re-educated those whose retraining task lies before them—that from these gonzo deadheads we must see increased devotion to all our causes or else they will give us the vast full pleasure of their demotion—that we here dryly devolve that the well-read shall not have tried Mark Twain—that this nation, under secular humanism, shall have a new burst of me-dom—and that punishment of the P.C., by the P.C., for the P.C., shall blot the nightmarish of planet earth.

George Bush: The Getty-Oil Address

Fourscore and seven million years ago, dinosaurs brought forth upon this planet a carbonization, conceived in geology and deposited in the proposition that all energy is created cheaper. We then got engaged in a kind and gentle war, testing whether my ratings, or any ratings so contrived, can long endure.

I'm all set to provide a great sound-bite of that war.... It is altogether fitting a show-stopper that I should do this. Who says I cannot postulate, cannot politic, cannot make TV commercials on this ground?... The world will little vote, in any November, for anything I say here. But it will never forget the Democrats who didn't want us to fight here....

It's Dan Rather for us to see here derogated in the great task-explaining here before us—that for these Saudi women toward whom our troops dared not share their full pleasure and devotion—that we here highly resolve that those women shall not drive in lanes—and that lubrication, underground, shall bring a new purse to Sheikdoms—and that arguments of the petrol, by the petrol, and for the petrol, shall not be bearish to their worth.

Budweiser: The Get-a-Beer Address

Four pours and seven beers ago, why did our fathers bring forth on this continent a new nation? Why was it conceived in liberty? Why did anybody dedicate themselves to the proposition that all men are created equal? Why did we ever get engaged in a civil war? Why does anybody endure questions this long?

Why Ask Why? Drink beer, guy!

You'll be met by a fabulous field of babes.... Don't be so twitting, you schlepper, you should know this. But in a larger sense, we cannot dissipate, we cannot intoxicate, you cannot swallow this down.... The babes will little note, nor long remember, anything you say here, but they can never forget what you drink here....

It is lager for you, so be here dedicated to the great flask remaining before you—that you empty the cans from which you can take the last fool's measure of the potion—that we here feel highly absolved, that drinkers of our suds shall not die in vans—that this potion, under prod, shall give a new girth and spreedom—and that bubblements of the potted, by the potted, for the potted, shall not be squarish, for what it's worth.

Guide to Vietnam-Era Draft Dodging

If you're a fortysomething male running for office, brace yourself! Back in the 60s, we'll bet you never thought the Vietnam-era draft would be a big political issue in the 90s. Then again, no one could have predicted that Dick Clark would look exactly the same today as he did then, or that Michael Jackson would turn Anglo-Saxon. So, as a public service, we offer this handy after-the-fact guide to 60s-era deferments and exemptions.

You remember these:

- 1-A: Tag! You're it!
- 1-O: Quakers and Shakers
- 1-Y: miscellaneous minor misfit
- 2-H: won lottery!
- 2-S: student deferment, free to chant: "Hell No, Somebody Else Go!"
- 3-A: job deferment (for teaching, preaching, Pentagon leeching)
- 3-C: Daddy Dearest
- 4-F: total wimpo wacko hippie misfit

Betcha didn't know about these:

- 1-DQ: disqualified (or Dan Quayle, on volleyball duty)
- 2-E: spits
- 2-CD: needs disinfectant
- 2-FT: costly to feed
- 2-RT: keeps painting the ceiling
- 2-X: pensive, travagant, otic
- 3-M: red tape, sticky
- 4-H: likes farm animals too much
- 4-I: bad eyesight
- 4-N: unAmerican
- 4-T: aging yuppie

For the next war, we hear the Pentagon is planning a brand new, 1990s-style draft, with a whole new list of deferments and exemptions, including:

A-1:	saucy
A-2:	Bru-te
A-1 and A-2:	accordion player
B-2:	invisible
B-TLS:	long-hair, English accent
R-2-D-2:	short, stupid robot
C-3-P-O:	tall, stupid robot
6-T-6:	on Medicare
8-2-MUCH:	indigestion
100-2-1:	odds against drafting Pete Rose
K-9:	a real dog
A-CHU:	hay fever
IQ-50:	married to first cousin
C-SICK:	not allowed on navy ships
YUP-E:	incapable of eating w/o cuisinart
PREP-E:	allergic to non-designer clothes
S-UNUNU:	cannot travel by bus or train
0–75:	Bingo!

"Seeing Action" During Nam

Stand by Your Mansion

Which of the following private residences should guide your political ambitions?

The White House

Big mansion near large river

Has one present resident, often seen elsewhere

Present resident earns $250,000/year

Resident wishes he could talk like a truck-driver

Site of wild parties in early 1960s

Suspicion surrounds accounts of 1963 resident's death, which millions still grieve

20 percent of current or former residents have their picture on a U.S. postage stamp

Graceland

Bigger mansion near larger river

Has one former resident, often seen elsewhere

Last resident earned $250,000,000/year

Last resident was a truck-driver

Site of wild parties in early 1960s

Suspicion surrounds accounts of 1977 resident's death, which billions still grieve

100 percent of current or former residents have their picture on a U.S. postage stamp

Political Ineptitude Test: History

1. World War II is to the Gulf War as D-Day is to:
   (a) Desert Storm
   (b) Hail Mary
   (c) Super Mario Brothers

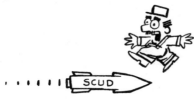

2. In the 1820s, President John Quincy Adams skinny-dipped in the Potomac. That practice was discontinued by later Presidents because:
   (a) Cameras were invented.
   (b) No one else has looked as cute from behind.
   (c) Palm Beach has warmer water.

3. Who does film director Oliver Stone believe actually did act alone?
   (a) Lee Harvey Oswald
   (b) Jack Ruby
   (c) Peewee Herman

4. Harry Truman is to the Marshall Plan as George Bush is to:
   (a) read my flips
   (b) the vision thing
   (c) selling Big Macs to the former Soviet Union

Shamlet

We now bring you the Shakespearean tragedy of Shamlet-on-the-Hudson, starring New York Governor Mario Cuomo.

Ac-Cen-Tchu-Ate the Negative!

While your Pharaoh has been busy building pyramids, all we hear Moses saying is "Thou shalt not this, thou shalt not that." And what about the one big thing he claims he did—making the Red Sea part? The fish industry is still paying for that blunder. And enough talk about a "promised land." Hey, Moses, take two tablets and call us in the morning. (paid for by the Committee to Elevate the Pharaoh to Sun God)

Why are Robin Hood's men so merry? You'd be merry, too, if you were hired under a quota system for thieves. That's right. You were the best-qualified for the job, but it went to a common criminal. And as if that weren't bad enough, he wants to return to the failed "trickle down" policies of the past. It's time to stop the robbin', hood. (paid for by the Committee to Re-Elect the Sheriff of Nottingham)

(Famous Attack Ads in History)

Look at this. Columbus says the earth is round. Shyeah, right!!! So what's the sky? A trapezoid? Here we are, with thousands of cobblers and bloodletters out of work, and he wants Spanish taxpayers to foot the bill for his sailing off the end of the earth. Reach India by sailing west? You believe that, an' I got a bridge in the "New World" to sell you. (paid for by the Committee to Preserve the Dark Ages)

This is a cherry tree. More to the point, this was a cherry tree. Next to it is an axe—George's axe. Think of the cherry tree as your future, just getting ready to blossom. Do you want some toothless, uneducated guy—a guy who throws coins across rivers, a guy who sleeps here, there, everywhere—to do to your future what he did to this cherry tree? (paid for by the Keep George III Your King Committee)

O Metzenbaum

Sung to the tune of "O Christmas Tree (O Tannenbaum)"

First Verse (English)

O Clarence T, O Clarence T's
Judicial Nomination
Turned out to be like trash TV
It entertained our nation
A bunch of silly Senate men
Exposed themselves on CNN
Judiciary, Judiciary
You big abomination

Second Verse (German)

O Metzenbaum, O Metzenbaum
Das Klareins Tomaus Heerink
Mit Bidenbum Und Specterbum
Dehrs Naht Ein Fraulein Cheerink
Komedienz Maehk Diertie Johks
Auf Silber Daung Und Hairzen Kohks
O Kennedy, O Kennedy
Bie Scheur Und Kipp Das Paentz Ohn

Political Ineptitude Test: Vocabulary

1. Define "WEEKEND" (Usage: Congress just recessed for the *weekend*.)
   (a) Saturday and Sunday
   (b) 5 PM Friday to 9 AM Monday
   (c) Thursday through Tuesday

2. Use the phrase "dumb and lazy American" in a sentence correctly.
   (a) I am a dumb and lazy American.
   (b) I ain't no dum and lazie American, you dweeb.
   (c) I would think of a sentence using the phrase "dumb and lazy American," but it would be too much of a hassle.

3. Define "WASTE" (Usage: There is too much government *waste*.)
   (a) Benefits you get, but don't need.
   (b) Benefits you get, but never paid for.
   (c) Benefits that somebody else gets.

4. If you tell a Dallas woman of Mexican ancestry that she reminds you of your ex-wife, you are guilty of:
   (a) Sexism   (c) Texism
   (b) Mexism   (d) Exism

5–12. Match the OXY with the MORON: (e.g., the words "Democratic" and "Leadership" can be combined to make the oxymoron "Democratic Leadership")

5. check and	(a) intelligence
6. ethics	(b) Rehnquist
7. legal	(c) environment
8. urban	(d) action
9. Justice	(e) memoirs
10. military	(f) committee
11. political	(g) balance
12. Reagan	(h) brief

Five-Iron Johns

(The five living men who have held the office of President held a Wild Man weekend retreat at Fort Drum....)

NIXON: Wow, it's getting hot in here! But to be a REAL man, you gotta take the heat. You gotta let 'em make you sweat — and you gotta have an enemies list.

BUSH: Golly, I just love this warm togetherness thing. Makes me want to be the "perspiration President." Start a whole "New World Odor."

CARTER: Can they turn down the thermostat? It's too hot to hug.

REAGAN: Well, there you go again, Jimmy. I want you to ask yourself, are you better off now than you were four hours ago? By the way, did you guys ever see "Tomcats of the Navy?" There was a lot of real sweaty male bonding in that.

CARTER: I'm here to share my primal fear of rabbits and find therapy for malaise. So far, all that helps is the tomahawk chop.

REAGAN: Well, let's suppose that you strongly suspect your wife is making time with some 77-year-old crooner with some tough-looking bodyguards, and you can't stay awake long enough to stop it. Whaddaya do?

BUSH: Don't know about this sensitive guy thing. What did it get Jimmy? Eighteen percent interest rates! I believe in low interest rates. Y'know, when it comes to domestic policy, I have a low interest rate.

CARTER: George, the rhythm of the drums can make us more sensitive guys. So then, if you don't have the slightest idea what you're doing, you can... (can I say this, guys?)... stop and ask directions.

FORD: All I am is just a success object, an attraction on a golf tournament marquee.

NIXON: Pardon me?

CARTER: OK, guys: This is a talking stick. (picks up charred branch) It gives the bearer the right to be heard without interruption, no matter how boring you are. Bill Clinton had one at the '88 convention, and Paul Tsongas had one this year. Because the stick compels you to speak, it encourages spontaneous and truthful outbursts. Jerry, you start us off.

FORD: (taking stick) Gosh, I do these golf events, and I get paid, and I feel terrible! Traveling from club to club, course to course, constantly hitting my head with my five-iron. It's like Rotary from Hell. Hey guys, gimme a hug!

REAGAN: (tapping stick on temple) Truth be told, I really fooled everybody! That Iran-Contra: I knew about it all. I'm a whiz at the complex details of international finance. Under that Teflon exterior is a steel-trap mind. And trickle down? What a scam! It sure trickled down to me, via the Japanese!

CARTER: (hugging stick) I lied to Playboy! I never felt lust in my heart! It was in my loins! The loins—

NIXON: (grabbing stick) OK! I AM a crook. Hey, George, what about you?

BUSH: Not gon' do it.... Not gon' do it.... (tries to run. Ford tackles him, and Carter crams stick into his hand.) A poem. By George Herbert Walker "Pappy" Bush.

the preppy screams, but no one hears
not even muffy
who mixes gin and tonics at the club
and yet the preppy knows the pain
of golf spikes too downtrodden
or plaids too muted to cry out
and alligators too green
and still the preppy screams
"FORE!"

REAGAN: That's not all, George. You'll get no photo-op from me until you tell it all.

BUSH: So many things kept to myself. Where to start? Quayle? Ohhhh Danny! WHAT WAS I THINKING? Breaking my "read my lips" pledge has to take a silver medal to that one. And want you to know, LOVE to travel, LOVE IT! Can't get enough of Princes, Kings, Dictators, NATO, SEATO, Eastern Europe, Moscow, China. HoJos in Peoria? Can't hold a candle. Sununu was right. Big thrill to jet away, often as I can.

CARTER: That's still not all, George.

BUSH: OK! OK! (waves stick) We've got a r, a re-, a recessssss—a RECESSION! IN A RECESSION! MAYBE DEPRESSION! (The five men conga out of the lodge.)

(A new group enters, having just completed a presidential candidate's debate. They strip down, and put on some paint. One of them picks up the stick.)

CLINTON: You already know about Gennifer and the ROTC. NOW lemme tell ya about....

The Daily Presidential Grind

If you are planning to become President (and, in some of your cases, for our country's sake, we hope this is not possible), you must learn to keep a daily schedule. As a public service, we are printing previously unpublished samples of the schedules of Presidents Bush and Reagan.

Bush

Daily Schedule

A.M.	6:00	wake up, go jogging
	7:00	try to board Air Force One, find Sununu has keys
	8:00	attend budget briefing, hear words like "deep doo doo"
	9:00	Chief of Staff "volunteers" to resign
	10:00	hold press conference to deny any knowledge of son, Neil
	11:00	preview physical fitness plan with Arnold Schwarzenegger

Reagan

Daily Schedule

A.M.	6:00	wake up, go back to sleep
	7:00	get bored by Air Force briefing, take nap
	8:00	attend budget briefing, hear words like "deep voo doo"
	9:00	Nancy "volunteers" to make Chief of Staff resign
	10:00	hold press conference to deny any knowledge of daughter, Patti
	11:00	preview "Kindergarten Cop" with Arnold Schwarzenegger

Bush

P.M.		
12:00	lunch; pork rinds, no broccoli	
2:00	say "read my lips, no new taxes"	
3:00	announce increase in taxes	
4:00	read poll, say raising taxes was big mistake	
5:00	play horseshoes while Bar entertains grandkids	
7:00	read bedtime story to Dan	
8:00	attend state dinner with Japanese prime minister	
8:05	photo op	
8:10	clean up	
8:15	send suit to cleaners	

Reagan

P.M.		
12:00	lunch; vegetable-du-jour ketchup, jellybeans	
2:00	say cutting taxes will cut deficit	
3:00	announce increase in deficit	
4:00	read poll, say cutting taxes was no mistake	
5:00	play President while Nancy entertains Frank Sinatra	
7:00	watch Bedtime for Bonzo	
8:00	attend state dinner with Japanese prime minister	
8:05	photo op	
8:10	clean up, obtain promise of $2 million speaking fee	
8:15	send country to cleaners	

Press? Your Pants, While-U-Wait

Remember how *The New York Times* was quick to publish the name of Willie Smith's accuser, and how a story leaked by *The Star* caused Bill Clinton to lose the New Hampshire primary? These days it's getting harder and harder to tell the sleazy tabloids from the hard-news papers.

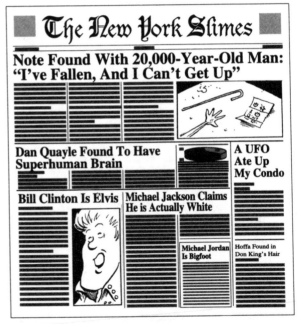

Political Ineptitude Test: Dan's World

1. Wayne is to Garth as George is to:
   - (a) Dan
   - (b) Quayle
   - (c) Dan Quayle

2. If you're Dan Quayle and are preparing to give a speech in Albany, you should first:
   - (a) Do research on local issues
   - (b) Find out where Albany is
   - (c) Learn to speak Albanian

3. If you're an incumbent who refers to himself as the "Education President," how can you win the youth vote?
   - (a) Show a real concern about the future
   - (b) Say "Balanced budget? As if!"
   - (c) Try to convince young voters that you're related to the family that brews Busch beer.

Lirty Dies

There is nothing worse than a sex scandal
Let me say that again
There is wuthing nurse than a skex sandal

My stirst fory is about that dealer wheeler, Tronald Dump
And his spuvely louse, Trissus Mump
When the Dumps were worst fed, they were mappily harried
But they signed a denuptial preal
Then Dump went on the trast fack, got rilthy fich, and met a Porgia jeech
It was his ducky lay!
Trissus Mump felt schnotally tookered, and Dump was in trig bubble
Trissus Mump isn't honey mungry
All she wants is the Plump Traza, the Bump Trilding, the Shump Truttle,
And the three Trittle Lumps
Chat fance, Trissus Mump!
Getting tro out of Dump
Is like taking stud from a blone
He doesn't have a pickle in his nocket!

TRONALD
DUMP

My stekond sory is about Kister Mennedy of Chassamusetts
Alias Tuncle Ed
The faterpamilias of the Clennedy Kan
Tuncle Ed is a laming fliberal — and one gorny hi!
So Tuncle Ed set-jetted to Balm Peach with a sephew and a nun
They went to a cligh-hass clite-nub
Where they chubble-dugged a few Warvey Ball-Hangers
Then Tuncle Ed said, "Hey! It's tarty pime!
Let's go to my heach bouse for a kite-nap!"
Along came those singing swingles,
Smillie With and Battie Powman
Here's what sea head and see shed by the she-sore
"Hey, Battie, let's go dinny-skipping!"
"Hey, Smillie, I've lost my hanty-pose!"
Then Batty got Smillie into trig bubble
After a trublic pile before a pury of his jeers
Smillie was found gotally not tilty!
And Tuncle Ed? He thill stinks he can be a shig bot
On the sore of the Flenate
Better keep his bousers truckled!

TUNCLE
ED

My stird fory is about America's cavorite fupple
Tarence Chlomas and Hanita Ill
Chlomas is a jederal fudge ... and a wite-ringer
Ill is a praw lofessor
Who claims she got warassed in the hurkplace
What a shirty dame!
When Ill went into her oss's boffice,
Here's what sea shed sea head (No she sore this time)
"Hey, bunny-honey, wanna dig bate?
Wanna hole in the ray?
Wanna see my song long dilver?
Hookey lear: There's something cubic on my poke!"
Ill was ossed grout!
In a hublic peering, she pe-reated his wirty dirds over all the wetnurks!
And those so-hard Blenators made Horrin Atches of themselves
We ought to take him and Tuncle Ed and make 'em Sex-Enators
So who's trelling the tooth ... and who's trelling the lirty die?
The nictim, or the vominee? Koo hares!
Chlomas is bepping up to the stench!
And Ill? Watch her bite a rook
And that rook is gonna make her bitch!

TARENCE
CHLOMAS

My storth fory is about that Cremodatic runt-frunner, Clill Binton
Clill was a roar wesister, a smot poker, and a wit of a bomanizer
Back in Riddle Lock, he met a quootie bean named Flennifer Jowers
What a rome-hecker!
Flennifer called up a teazy grabloid
And said she was Clill's tot hicket
Now Clill is in lig bimbo!
So he went on the tube-boob with his house, Spillary
That Spillary is no Wammy Tynette!
But, hey Clill, you're no K.F.J.!
Neither is that Kob Berrey and his Webby Dinger!
Or Saul Pongas, that meek from Grassachusetts!
The one who's biling is Smush
If you wanna get pricked for pesident,
You gotta be a hoar wearo —
And a sponogamous mouse!

The storal of my mories is this:
If you ever get in a skex sandal, watch out:
You'll deceive what you reserve!

CLILL
BINTON

Final Exit: A How-To Guide to Political Suicide

Eventually, you may find political life too unbearable, or you may find yourself about to be killed off by a well-funded opponent. If so, you might consider committing POLITICAL SUICIDE. This is so easy to do, even Walter Mondale was able to do it. He used DEATH BY TAXES. But you may prefer a less horrible method.

Death by Automobile

Here's a quick and painless way to go. Simply drive your Toyota to a United Auto Workers rally.

Death by Handgun

This one's a bit messy, but usually requires only a 7-day waiting period. All you have to do is oppose the NRA.

Death by Foreign Government

This isn't a bad way to go, since it requires extensive foreign travel to exotic places. Just promise that you will send billions in aid to former Soviet republics and the Third World.

Death by Fatty Foods

Clog your fund-raising arteries until you choke by telling wealthy beef, pork, and dairy farmers: "Your subsidies are a big rip-off to taxpayers, and your price supports are an even bigger rip-off to consumers."

Death by High-Tech Weapon

This is for the economy-minded. Announce that you oppose a high-tech defense weapons system in your district. An explosion will follow.

Death by Nuclear Annihilation

Just say "I support nuclear power," and wait for the fallout.

Death by Old Age

A time-tested way to go. Ask your spin doctors to disconnect you from your life-support political machines, and you'll go quickly. Simply say "let's tax Social Security benefits that go to rich people."

New World Borders

Political Ineptitude Test: Geography

1. The correct new name for the former U.S.S.R. is:

    (a) The U.S.S.-Were

    (b) The Commonwealth of Semi-Associated Quasi-Independent Mega-Nuclear States

    (c) Big Place Next to Finland

2. What is the official new flag of Russia?

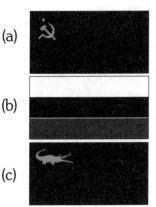

3. In Washington, D.C., the most famous monument inscription is:

    (a) "George Washington Slept Here." (Mt. Vernon)

    (b) "Ronald Reagan Slept Here." (White House, Oval Office)

    (c) "Frank Sinatra Slept Here." (White House, Lincoln Bedroom)

4. What does the U.S. trade the most frequently with Japan?

    (a) microchips

    (b) baseball players

    (c) insults

Still going...

Are You Fit? Enter the PIT!

Dear POLITICAL INEPTITUDE TEST Contestant:

Before we instruct you how to enter the PIT, we are required by the Federal Commission of Statistical Techno-Geeks to ask the following question:

Did you cheat?   YES ❑   YES, BUT I DIDN'T GET CAUGHT ❑

To enter the PIT, fill out both sides of the 2-page answer form: the multiple choice questions, and the essay questions. FOR GOD'S SAKE, USE A NUMBER TWO PENCIL!!! (we have no idea why) — and mail it to:

INEPT JUDGES
THE CAPITOL STEPS
1505 KING STREET
ALEXANDRIA, VA 22314

If the inept judges find you unfit, we'll send you a certificate, suitable for a frame-up, designating you as a Certified Fool fully capable of replacing the real FOOLS ON THE HILL!

Like the Fools themselves, the inept judges retain the right to be totally capricious.

PIT Answer Form Part I: Multiple Choice Questions

Congress Maze _____

Current Events ___(1) ___(2) ___(3) ___(4) ___(5)

Congre-Gorian ___ ___ ___ ___ ___
Calendar ___ ___ ___ ___ ___
___

Movies ___(1) ___(2) ___(3) ___(4) ___(5)
___(6) ___(7) ___(8)

No Santa ___(1) ___(2) ___(3) ___(4) ___(5)
Claus ___(6) ___(7) ___(8)

Math ___(1) ___(2) ___(3) ___(4)

Politically Correct ___(1) ___(2) ___(3) ___(4) ___(5)
Sports Team ___(6) ___(7) ___(8) ___(9) ___(10)
Names ___(11) ___(12) ___(13) ___(14) ___(15)

Ethics ___(1) ___(2) ___(3) ___(4) ___(5)

Politics ___(1) ___(2) ___(3) ___(4) ___(5)

History ___(1) ___(2) ___(3) ___(4)

Vocabulary ___(1) ___(2) ___(3) ___(4) ___(5)
___(6) ___(7) ___(8) ___(9) ___(10)
___(11) ___(12)

Dan's World ___(1) ___(2) ___(3)

Geography ___(1) ___(2) ___(3) ___(4)

Check your answers for "Many a Cross Word" here.
Did you get them right? _____ Really? _____

PIT Answer Form Part II: Essay Questions

Suppose you're running for Congress. What's your campaign slogan? _____

_____

Describe in detail your plans for achieving global peace and prosperity. Give specifics. Do not exceed 25 words.

_____ _____ _____ _____ _____ _____ _____ _____

_____ _____ _____ _____ _____ _____ _____ _____

_____ _____ _____ _____ _____ _____ _____

Write a (funny) negative ad your opponent may run against you, based on true facts about your life:

_____

_____

_____

Suppose, when running for re-election, you're pilloried by the press for (a) having bounced 999 checks; (b) losing your pants; (c) never returning to your home district. What's your excuse? _____

_____

_____

Who has been the funniest candidate of this election year? _____

Name: _____

Address: _____

I am entering the PIT. Let me know if I am a Certified Fool, capable of replacing the real FOOLS ON THE HILL.

Signature: _____ Date: _____

About the Capitol Steps

The Capitol Steps began in 1981, at a Christmas party in the office of Senator Charles Percy. The original cast had intended to put on a traditional nativity play. But in the entire Congress, they couldn't find three wise men or a virgin!

Now, more than a decade later, the Steps perform more than 300 shows a year—at Chelsea's (their Washington showcase) and on tour all across America. Their live shows consist mainly of song parodies, with a cast of five, a pianist, and several bags of props. They have recorded 11 albums, are featured in periodic comedy specials on PBS-TV and National Public Radio, and can be regularly seen on the Today Show, Good Morning America, CNN, and other news and entertainment programs. Presidents Reagan and Bush have each personally been the targets of Capitol Steps roastings at the White House.

All the Steps performers have worked on Capitol Hill, some for Democrats and some for Republicans. They believe that our political system

LEFT: Brian Ash, Dave Gencarelli, Anne Willis Hill, Jim Aidala.
RIGHT: Mike Loomis, Emily Bell Spitz, Helen Gleason, Bo Ayars.

can be explained very simply: The Republicans goof up, and the Democrats party. Then the Democrats goof up, and the Republicans party. That's what the Capitol Steps call the two-party system.

The book text is the handiwork of Bill Strauss (pictured below, right) and Elaina Newport (below, left), with contributions from Dave Werner. Strauss and Newport are the co-writers of Capitol Steps song lyrics, and (with Jim Aidala) co-founders of the troupe. Newport is the Steps' Producer, Strauss the Director, Werner a Steps performer. The cartoons are by R.J.Matson, whose work can be seen in *Roll Call* and *The New York Observer,* and on numerous Capitol Steps record album covers.

LEFT: Sonya Pleasant Roth, Mike Tilford, Duncan Hollomon, Richard Paul. MIDDLE: Elaina Newport, Bill Strauss. RIGHT: Dave Werner, Ann Schmitt, Amy Felices Young, cartoonist R.J. Matson.

To Order The Musical Political Satire of the Capitol Steps:

If you liked The Book, you'll love The Movie—er ah, we mean our cassettes, CDs, and LPs. Eleven, to be exact.

We especially recommend our most recent album, appropriately entitled "FOOLS ON THE HILL," which contains 21 song parodies, including "If I Weren't a Rich Man," "The Tsounds of Tsongas," "Stand By Your Klan," and "Superfranticunproductivenothinglegislation."

But wait! There's more! Check out our other albums of the 1990s: "76 BAD LOANS," "SHEIK, RATTLE & ROLL," and "GEORGIE ON MY MIND." And for a look at the prehysterical 1980s, get the rest of our collection.

First cassette/LP:..$10
Each additional cassette/LP: $5
Complete set of 11 cassettes: $55

First CD: $12
Each additional CD: $8
Complete set of 7 CDs: $55

Postage/Handling: please add $3 for orders of $20 and under; add $5 for orders over $20.
Virginia residents please add 4.5% sales tax.

❑ **YES, I'M FIGHTING THE RECESSION! I'M BUYING MADE-IN-AMERICA POLITICAL SATIRE!**

Enclosed is a check for $_____ for the items marked on the back of this page. Would you like fries with that?_____

NAME:_____

STREET ADDRESS: _____

CITY/STATE/ZIP _____

TELEPHONE (_____) _____

And going and going...

"FOOLS ON THE HILL" (songs of 1992) CASSETTE ❏ CD ❏
(If I Weren't a Rich Man, Tsounds of Tsongas, Red Rubber Checks, God Bless My Chevrolet, Stand By Your Klan, Can't Love Helpin' That Man of Mine, Tax Your Children Well, Superfranticunproductivenothinglegislation, Lirty Dies, and more)

"76 BAD LOANS" (songs of 1991) CASSETTE ❏ CD ❏
(Fun, Fun, Fun 'Til Teddy Puts His T-Shirt Away, Atsa Lawyer, Lookin' for Scuds in All the Wrong Places, I Feel Petty, and more)

"SHEIK, RATTLE & ROLL" (songs of 1990) CASSETTE ❏ CD ❏
(Camel Lot, K-K-Kuwaitis, Who'll Put a Bomb on Saddam Saddam Saddam, Read My Flips, Leader of the P.A.C., We Arm the World, and more)

"GEORGIE ON MY MIND" (songs of 1990) CASSETTE ❏ CD ❏
(Talk Like a Dan, What's the Matter with Reds Today?, You Light Up My Flag, Yes We Have No-Riega, Your Statue Needs a Tu-Tu, and more)

"DANNY'S FIRST NOEL" (holiday songs) CASSETTE ❏ CD ❏
(We Need a Little Isthmus, I Saw Mommy Kissing Gorbachev, 'Twas the Night Before Recess, Ronald the Red-Faced Reagan, and more)

"STAND BY YOUR DAN" (songs of 1989) CASSETTE ❏ CD ❏
(Tanks for the Memories, I've Grown Accustomed to This Base, September Seventh, Life's a Beach, Mergermania, Gorby Gorbachev, and more)

"SHAMLET" (songs of 1988) CASSETTE ❏ LP ❏
(Ducoccus, Hartbreak Hotel, Biden Time, Little Doc Koop, Holy Rollercoaster, Downside Story, Ollie Would, and more)

"WORKIN' 9 TO 10" (songs of 1987) CASSETTE ❏ LP ❏
(Bomb Tehran Tehran, Hart Attack, Mighty Casey and the Spooks, Car Wars, Fatal Distractions, The Supremes, and more)

"THANK GOD I'M A CONTRA BOY" (songs of 1986) CASSETTE ❏ LP ❏
(We Circled France All Night, Libya O Libya, the Meesekateers, Bye Bye Burger, Mr. Rehnquist's Neighborhood, The Frill is Gone, and more)

""WE ARM THE WORLD" (songs of 1985) CASSETTE ❏ LP ❏
(Dutch the Magic Reagan, You Write Up My Wife, Get Me to the Dirge on Time, Mama Don't Let Your Babies Grow Up to be Yuppies, and more)

"THE CAPITOL STEPS! LIVE!" (songs of 1984) CASSETTE ❏ LP ❏
(The Wreck of the Walter Fritz Mondale, The Great Defender, Immense Expense is Mainly in Defense, Mutual Annihilation Society, and more)